From Your MAILBOX®

FEBRUARY

A MONTH OF REPRODUCIBLES AT YOUR FINGERTIPS!

Kindergarten

Editor:
Angie Kutzer

Writers:
Susan Bunyan, Lucia Kemp Henry, Angie Kutzer

Art Coordinator:
Clevell Harris

Artists:
Cathy Spangler Bruce, Clevell Harris, Sheila Krill,
Mary Lester, Rob Mayworth, Barry Slate

Cover Artist:
Jennifer Tipton Bennett

www.themailbox.com

©1998 by THE EDUCATION CENTER, INC.
All rights reserved.
ISBN #1-56234-226-6

Manufactured in the United States

10 9 8 7 6 5 4

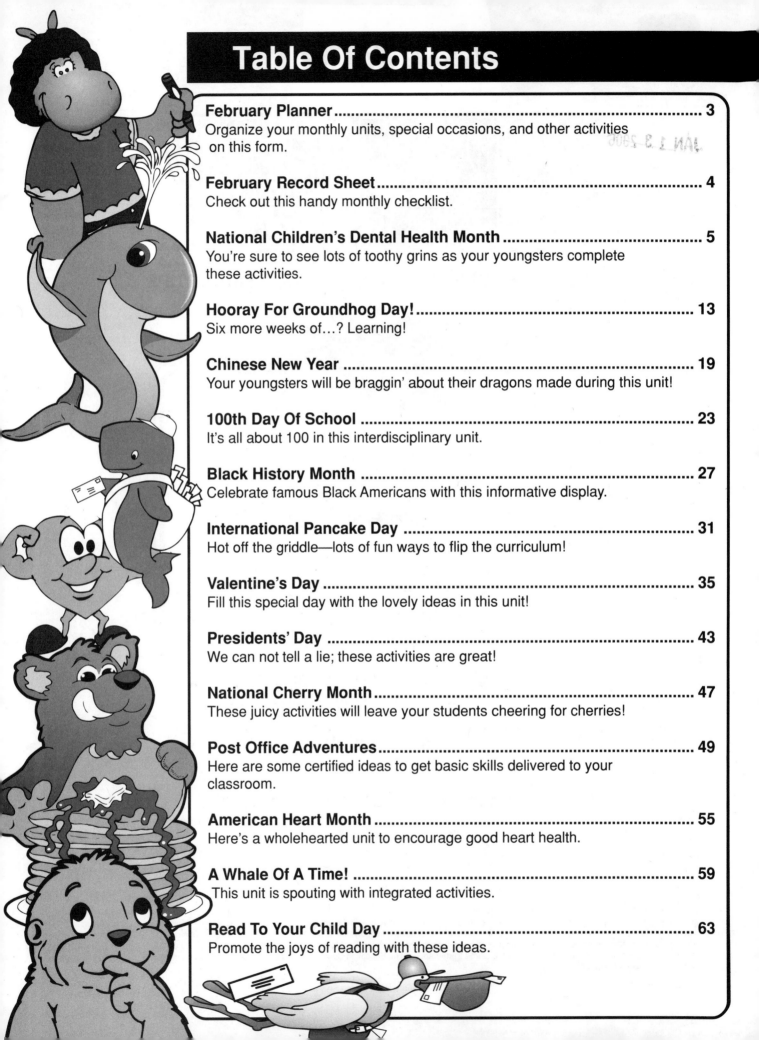

Table Of Contents

Books To Check Out:

To Do:

FEBRUARY
Classroom Themes:

Special Dates:

Meetings:

Materials To Collect:

Duties This Month:

Birthdays:

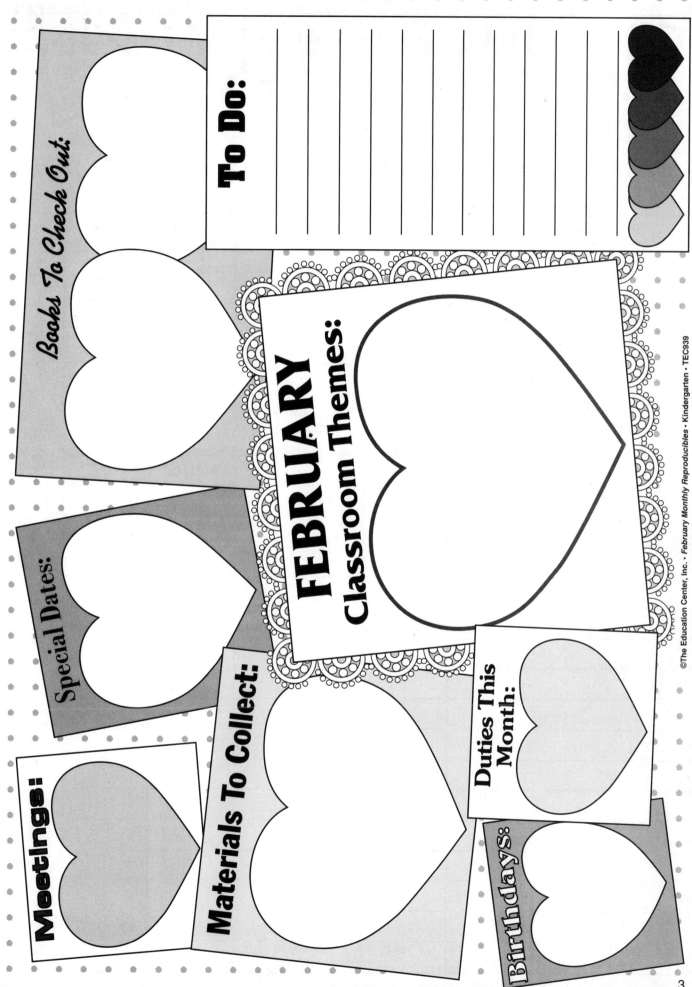

FEBRUARY

National CHILDREN'S DENTAL HEALTH Month

Your students will be all smiles when you use these dental health activities to celebrate National Children's Dental Health Month in February. Reinforce healthy teeth habits as you help youngsters brush up on a few skills from across the curriculum.

All Aboard!

Help your youngsters make these "chew-chew" trains to review the three most important aspects of proper dental care: *diet, daily cleaning,* and *regular checkups.* Duplicate pages 7–10 onto construction paper for each child. Read through the following instructions and gather the necessary materials for each child. (For ease in organization, you may want to give students only one page at a time to complete.) For each page, have the child color and cut out the train piece. Read aloud and discuss the text; then help the child complete each page as follows:

Engine (page 7): Write your name in the space provided; then color, cut out, and glue the missing pieces onto the engine.
First Boxcar (page 8): Color, cut out, and glue the healthful snacks to the boxcar.
Second Boxcar (page 9): Glue a length of dental floss in between the two fingers as shown; then squirt a short line of puffy fabric paint to resemble toothpaste on the toothbrush. Record a week's worth of brushing and flossing on the chart.
Caboose (page 10): Color and cut out the corresponding circle piece. Cut out the space indicated on the caboose. Secure the circle to the back of the caboose by inserting a brad fastener through the boldfaced Xs.

When all of the pages are finished, help each child use brads to connect his train together. Read the rhyming text again; then encourage each child to take his train home and share the dental basics with his family.

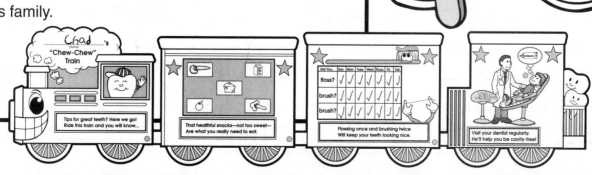

5

Types Of Teeth

Show your youngsters a diagram of human teeth. Point out the three different types of teeth: *incisors, canines,* and *molars.* Explain that each type has a specific purpose: the incisors are for biting and cutting, the canines are for tearing, and the molars are for grinding. Pass around several hand mirrors and encourage each child to try to locate each of the three types of teeth in her own mouth. Share the fact that types of teeth animals have are linked to what they eat. For example, giraffes have many broad, flat molars for grinding plants; lions have big canines to help them tear meat; and sharks have many of the same type of tooth to help them catch their prey. After this discussion, distribute a copy of page 11 to each child. Have her cut and paste the correct animal to its correct tooth structure. Chomp, chomp, chomp!

canine   molar
incisor

Cashing In

Use youngsters' excitement over lost teeth and the tooth fairy to practice money skills. After children have had an opportunity to share personal stories about the tooth fairy, direct them to close their eyes while you put several pennies under a pillow. Invite a volunteer to look under the pillow and tell the group how much money the tooth fairy left her. Continue until each child has had a turn. To vary the activity in order to work on coin recognition, leave one coin under the pillow and have the child tell the group whether the tooth fairy left her a penny, nickel, dime, or quarter. Follow up this activity with the reproducible on page 12.

Look, No Cavities!

Watch smiles light up the classroom as students play this toothy game. To prepare, purchase a bag of white beans. Use a marker to draw black dots (cavities) on several of the beans (teeth); then put all of the beans in a paper lunch bag. To play the game, pass the bag around the circle and have each child, without looking, pull out a tooth. If the tooth is clean, instruct the child to keep it. If the tooth has a cavity, the child returns the tooth—along with all the other teeth he has collected—back into the bag. Play continues until a child has collected a specified number of teeth.

's
_____
(Name)

"Chew-Chew"
Train

Tips for great teeth? Here we go!
Ride this train and you will know…

X

©1998 The Education Center, Inc. • *February Monthly Reproducibles* • Kindergarten • TEC939

Train Pattern
Use with "All Aboard!" on page 5.

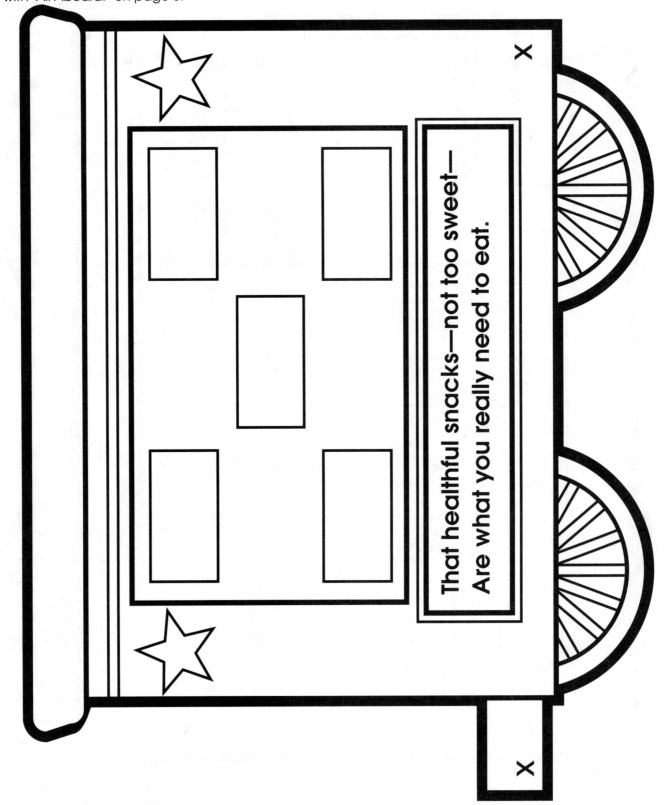

That healthful snacks—not too sweet—
Are what you really need to eat.

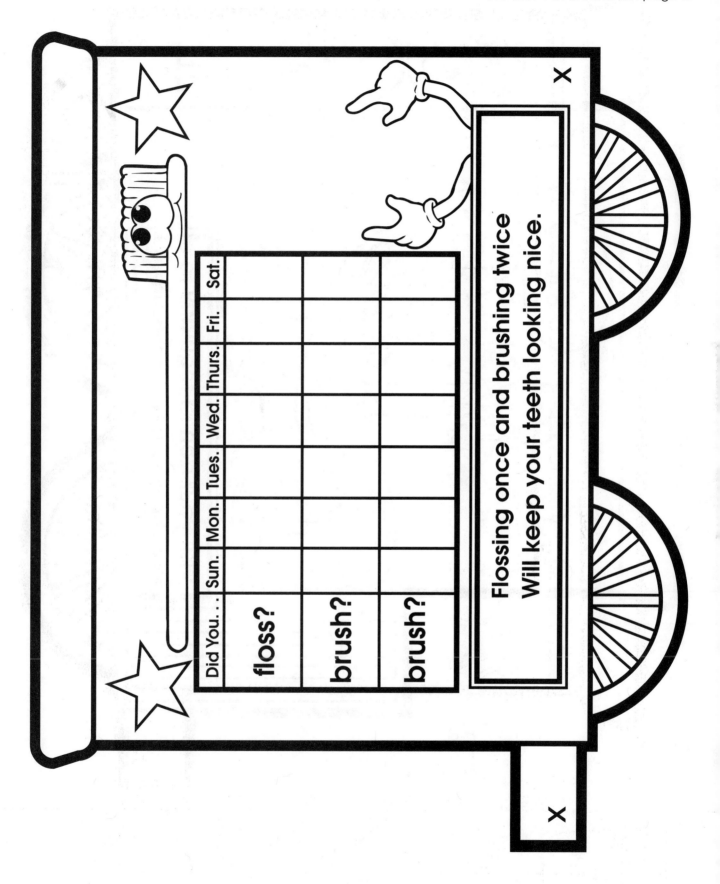

Did You...	Sun.	Mon.	Tues.	Wed.	Thurs.	Fri.	Sat.
floss?							
brush?							
brush?							

Flossing once and brushing twice
Will keep your teeth looking nice.

Train Pattern
Use with "All Aboard!" on page 5.

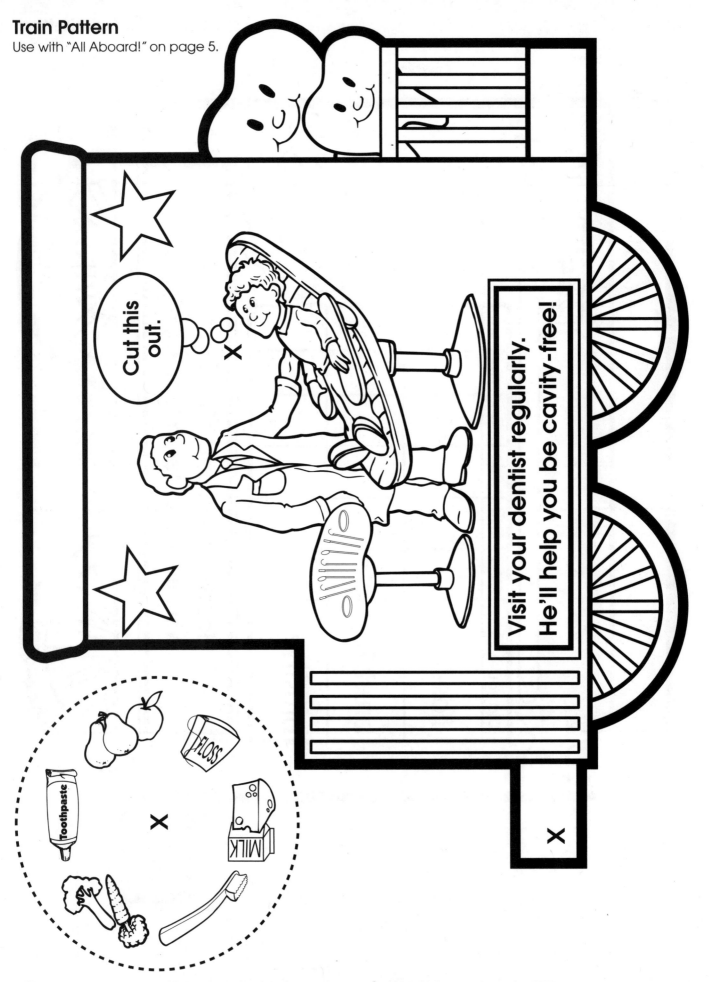

Cut this out.

Visit your dentist regularly. He'll help you be cavity-free!

Teeth Are Tools

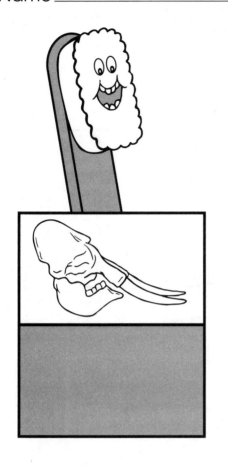

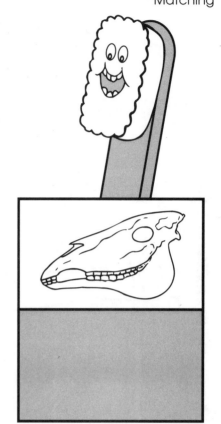

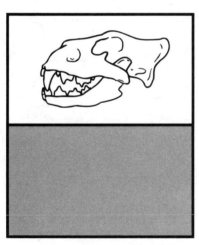

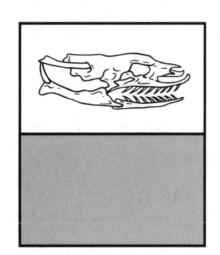

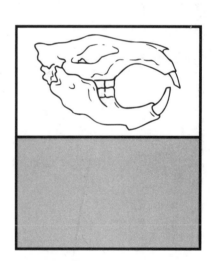

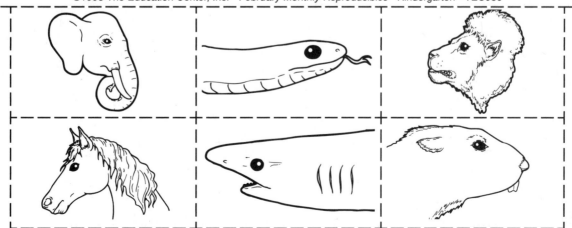

"Cent-sational" Teeth!

Count the number of pennies on each pillow.
Write the amount on the corresponding tooth.

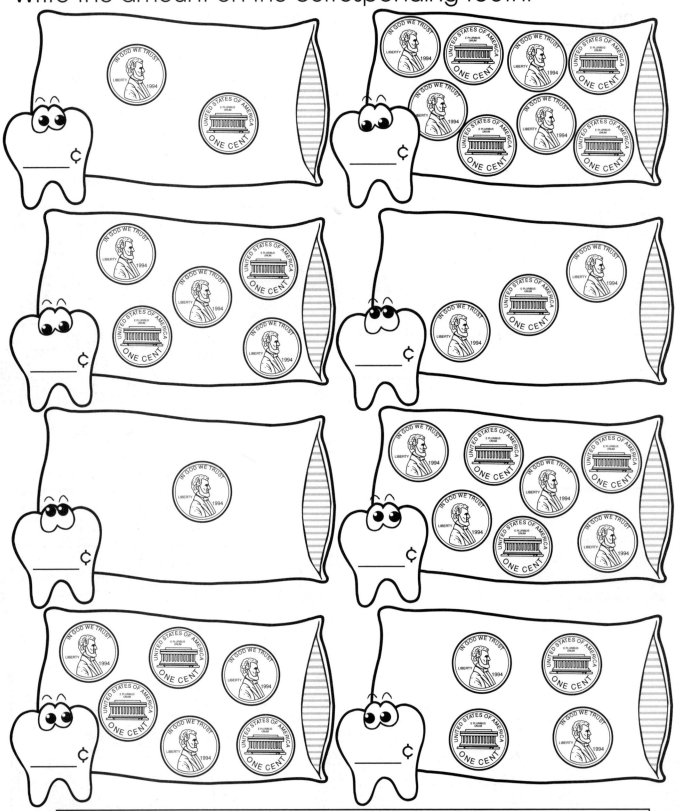

Bonus Box: What do you think the tooth fairy looks like? Draw one on the back of your paper.

©1998 The Education Center, Inc. • *February Monthly Reproducibles* • Kindergarten • TEC939

Hooray For Groundhog Day!

The predictions are in—these activities will turn winter blahs into spring fever, thanks to Mr. Groundhog!

Come On Out!

Sunny days bring shadows that your youngsters *don't* want to see as they play this game to get Mr. Groundhog out of his burrow. To prepare, duplicate the gameboard halves on pages 14 and 15. Color them, cut them out, and glue them side by side onto a large sheet of construction paper. Next make four construction-paper copies of the playing cards and groundhog marker on page 16. Color the pieces; then laminate the pages and the gameboard for durability. Cut out the cards and the groundhog markers. If desired, make the groundhogs stand by inserting each one into a section cut from a cardboard tube, as shown.

To play the game, shuffle the cards and place them in a pile facedown. Put a groundhog for each player (or use only one groundhog for a noncompetitive game) in the burrow. Draw a card. If the card has a cloud, your groundhog doesn't see his shadow, so move him forward one space. If the card has a sun, your groundhog sees his shadow, so move him backward one space. Continue taking turns until one player's groundhog makes it out of the tunnel (or until you've cooperatively moved one groundhog to the surface). For added difficulty, add numerals to the cards. No shadow is the way to go!

I Predict

Shed some light on sequencing with this activity. Duplicate page 17 for each child. Have her color the first two pictures that show the groundhog waking up and peeking out of his hole. Then have her color two of the remaining four pictures in order to show her prediction of whether or not the groundhog will see his shadow and the result of seeing it or not seeing it—more winter or early spring. Direct her to cut out the four colored pictures and glue them sequentially onto a strip of construction paper. To extend this activity, sort the students' strips into two groups: *shadow* and *no shadow*. Then compare the groups to see which one has the most strips. Will it be an early spring?

Other Weather Watchers

Don't let the groundhogs have all the fun! Encourage your youngsters to think of other possible weather watchers and predictions they could make. Give each child a copy of page 18 and have him illustrate his animal choice, then dictate a creative weather prediction in the space provided.

13

Gameboard

Use with "Come On Out!" on page 13.

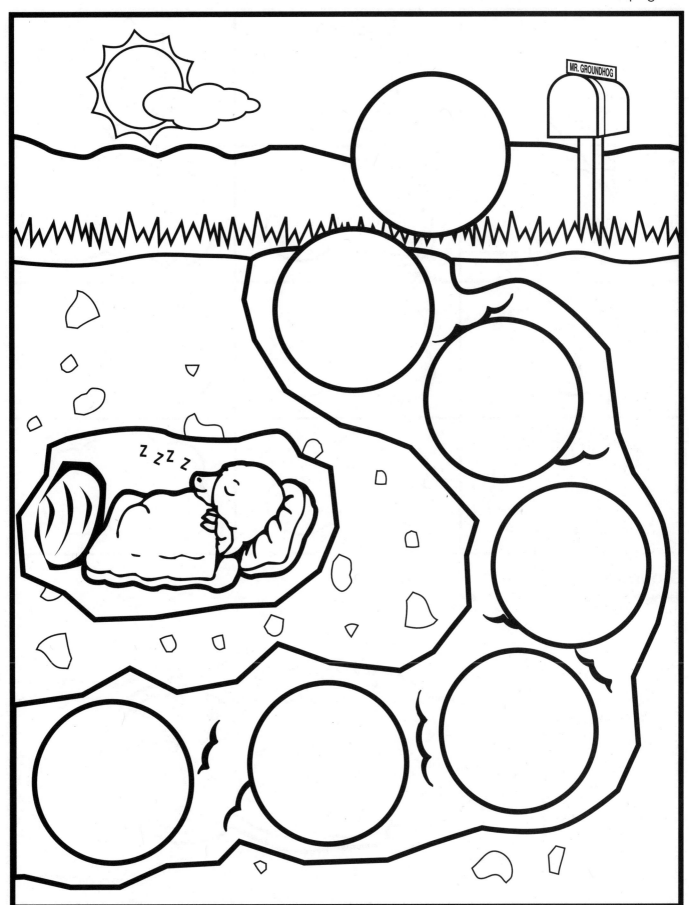

Game Cards
Use with "Come On Out!" on page 13.

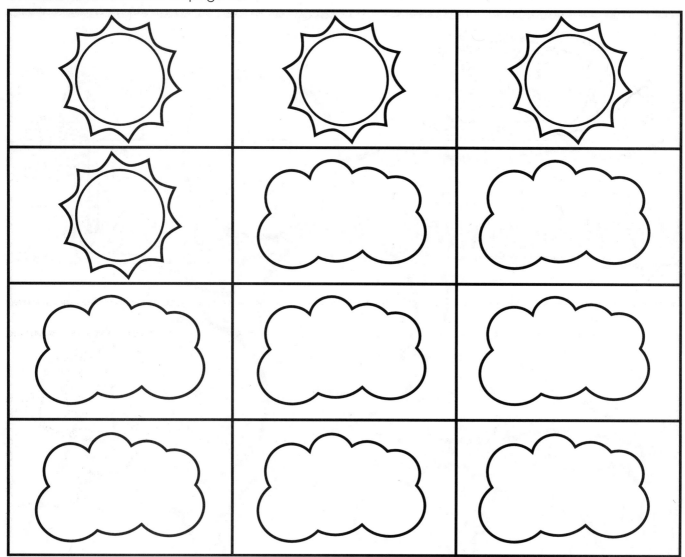

Groundhog Marker
Use with "Come On Out!" on page 13.

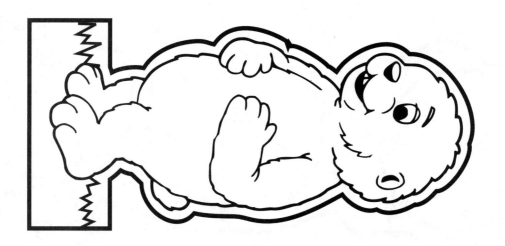

If a _____

sees its shadow,...

CHINESE NEW YEAR

"Gung Hay Fat Choy!" That's the traditional shout you'll hear during the annual Chinese New Year celebrations around the world. Use the information and activities below to encourage your youngsters to join the Chinese in perking up those February days that seem to be "dragon" by!

Chinese New Year

The New Year celebration is a major event on the Chinese calendar. The festivities begin somewhere between January 1 and February 19—depending on the old Chinese lunar calendar—and last about two weeks. While those living in China now celebrate the New Year with quiet celebrations at home because of the Chinese government's disapproval of the old customs, the Chinese abroad have huge celebrations complete with lion dances, firecrackers, and dragon parades.

Customary Rituals

Discuss some of the following Chinese New Year rituals with your students; then invite them to participate in the related classroom activities:

- *Before the New Year, clean your home very well to get rid of the bad luck that has accumulated during the past year.* What better excuse? Now's the time to encourage a little teamwork to get the classroom all tidied up.
- *Using a knife during the first days of the New Year will "cut off" good luck.* Challenge your youngsters not to use scissors for a few days.
- *Older family members give children red (considered a lucky color that protects against evil spirits) envelopes filled with money for prosperity.* On the last day of your Chinese New Year unit, treat each youngster with a red envelope filled with candy and play money.

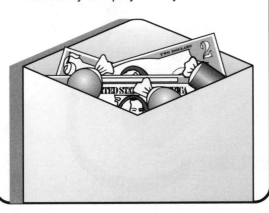

Here Come The Dragons!

The grand finale of the New Year celebration is the dragon parade, which usually ends in a burst of fireworks. It was believed long ago that the dragon controlled the clouds, rain, and rivers. Now the dragon dance is used to celebrate the spring rain and the sun. San Francisco hosts the biggest dragon parade in the world!

Fill your youngsters with the spirit of the Chinese New Year by making these dragon puppets and holding your own dragon parade—complete with plenty of noisemakers!

Materials For Each Child:
- 1 red construction-paper copy of the dragon head patterns on pages 20 and 21
- 1 construction-paper copy of the wing patterns on page 22
- 1 paper lunch bag
- several crepe-paper or fabric streamers in assorted colors and lengths
- colorful curling-ribbon pieces
- access to a stapler
- scissors
- glitter
- glue

Directions:
1. Cut out the head and wing pieces.
2. Decorate the pieces with glitter.
3. Glue one head and one wing piece to each side of the bag as shown.
4. Staple the front edges of the head pieces together.
5. Staple streamers around the open end of the bag.
6. Glue pieces of curling ribbon along the dragon's back.

Dragon Head Pattern

Use with "Here Come The Dragons!" on page 19.

Dragon Wing Patterns

Use with "Here Come The Dragons!" on page 19.

100th DAY OF SCHOOL

You made it! Now what are you going to do to celebrate? Use these activities and reproducibles to get the party started. Your students will be having so much fun, they won't even realize they're practicing some important basic skills!

Hunting For One Hundred

Send your youngsters on a Hundred Hunt to reinforce classifying, tallying, and recording data. Reproduce a copy of the chart on page 24 for each small group of students. Then bury ten of each of the pictured objects on the chart in your sand table. Invite one group of students to hunt at a time. (To speed up the process, you might want to prepare two or three more hunt sites in large, plastic storage tubs.) Direct one student to be the Recorder while the other group members dig to find the objects. Have the Recorder use tally marks on the chart to keep up with how many of each object have been found. Stop the group periodically and have children switch jobs until everyone has had a chance to be the Recorder. At the end of the hunt, have the children check themselves by sorting their objects and counting to make sure there are ten in each group.

One Hundred Hugs?

You bet! Read aloud a huggable story such as *A Hundred Hugs* by Joy Cowley (The Wright Group) or *Little Blue And Little Yellow* by Leo Lionni (Astor-Honor Publishing, Inc.). Give each child a copy of the record sheet on page 25; then challenge your little ones to find 100 people who need hugs (or several people who need more than one hug each). Explain to the child that after he gives someone a hug, he is to ask that person to sign his record sheet. When each child fills his sheet with 100 names, encourage him to return it to you for a treat—a handful of Hershey's® Hugs®!

A Puzzling Picture

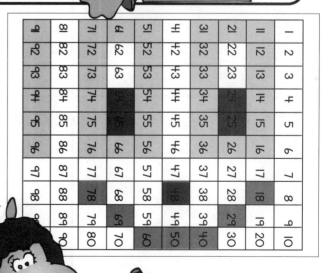

Your little detectives can crack the mystery of the puzzling picture *if* they can recognize numerals. Reproduce a class supply of the one-hundred grid on page 26. Have each child color her grid according to the following oral directions. For less difficulty, list the numerals that need to be colored on flash cards and use them to cue students. For greater difficulty, mix up the color groups and call out the numerals in random order. For example, "Color 16 purple. Color 78 red. Color 71 purple." After everyone has finished coloring, instruct each student to turn her grid sideways (clockwise) to reveal the hidden picture.

Directions:
1. Color the following numerals red: 18, 29, 40, 50, 60, 69, 78.
2. Color the following numerals black: 24, 25, 48, 64, 65.
3. Color the following numerals purple: 11–16, 21, 26, 31–36, 51–56, 61, 66, 71–76, 91–96.

Chart

Use with "Hunting For One Hundred" on page 23.

Hunting For One Hundred!	buttons	beans
crayons	linking cubes	pasta
paper clips	craft sticks	pom-poms
pipe cleaners	puzzle pieces	Group:

Name _____

I Gave 100 Hugs!

1._____	36._____	
2._____	37._____	
3._____	38._____	
4._____	39._____	
5._____	40._____	
6._____	41._____	71._____
7._____	42._____	72._____
8._____	43._____	73._____
9._____	44._____	74._____
10._____	45._____	75._____
11._____	46._____	76._____
12._____	47._____	77._____
13._____	48._____	78._____
14._____	49._____	79._____
15._____	50._____	80._____
16._____	51._____	81._____
17._____	52._____	82._____
18._____	53._____	83._____
19._____	54._____	84._____
20._____	55._____	85._____
21._____	56._____	86._____
22._____	57._____	87._____
23._____	58._____	88._____
24._____	59._____	89._____
25._____	60._____	90._____
26._____	61._____	91._____
27._____	62._____	92._____
28._____	63._____	93._____
29._____	64._____	94._____
30._____	65._____	95._____
31._____	66._____	96._____
32._____	67._____	97._____
33._____	68._____	98._____
34._____	69._____	99._____
35._____	70._____	100._____

1	2	3	4	5	6	7	8	9	10
11	12	13	14	15	16	17	18	19	20
21	22	23	24	25	26	27	28	29	30
31	32	33	34	35	36	37	38	39	40
41	42	43	44	45	46	47	48	49	50
51	52	53	54	55	56	57	58	59	60
61	62	63	64	65	66	67	68	69	70
71	72	73	74	75	76	77	78	79	80
81	82	83	84	85	86	87	88	89	90
91	92	93	94	95	96	97	98	99	100

BLACK HISTORY MONTH

Use these resources and activities to help your youngsters honor the contributions and achievements of African-Americans. Since 1976, the entire month of February has been designated Black History Month and is celebrated in schools, towns, and cities all across the United States.

Additional Resources

Use these excellent sources to enrich your youngsters' knowledge about renowned Black Americans from the past and present.

Biography Today
Edited by Laurie L. Harris
Published by Omnigraphics, Inc.

Follow In Their Footsteps
Written by Glennette Tilley Turner
Published by Cobblehill Books

African Americans Who Were First
Written by Joan Potter
and Constance Claytor
Published by Dutton Children's Books

Great African Americans Series
Outstanding African Americans Series
Published by Crabtree Publishing
Company

*Afro-Bets® Book Of Black Heroes
From A To Z*
Written by Wade Hudson
and Valerie Wilson Wesley
Published by Just Us Books, Inc.

Great American Displays

Create a gallery of positive personalities to highlight your youngsters' studies during Black History Month. Make tagboard copies of the display patterns on pages 28–30 for each child. Direct each student to cut out his patterns. Then help him glue the side panels behind the center panel as indicated. After reading about and discussing a wide variety of Black Americans—from political leaders, to inventors, to celebrities—ask each child to choose a different person to highlight on his display. Enlist the help of your media specialist, parents, volunteers, or older students to pair up with your children and help them research their chosen subjects. To complete the display, direct each child to write his subject's name on the left panel, draw and color a picture of his subject on the center panel, and dictate a fact about the person for the right panel. Invite each child to share the information on his display with the class. Then fold the panels of each display forward so that it stands alone. Arrange the displays on a tabletop and invite others to visit the gallery and learn more about some famous Black Americans.

Honor
Black Americans

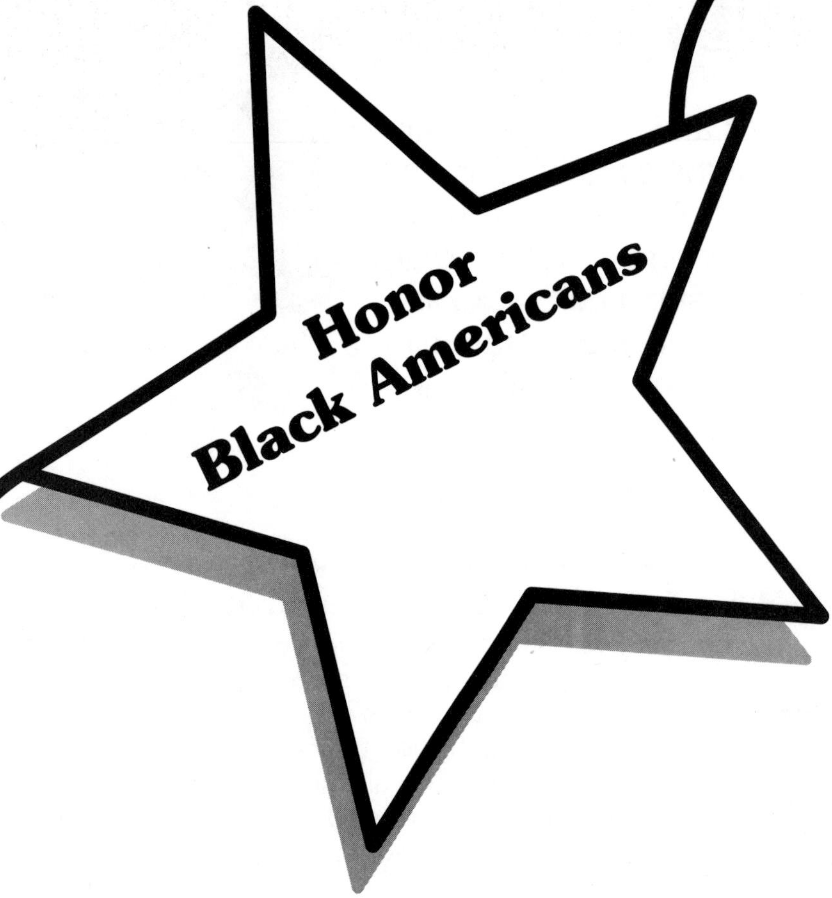

Glue behind left side of center section.

All About

_____

_____

by _____

A Great American

Glue behind right side of center section.

Black History Month

Did you know that

INTERNATIONAL PANCAKE DAY

Serve up this stack of basic-skills practice that uses those delectable breakfast favorites. Students will flip over these piping-hot activities. Come and get 'em!

Pancakes Plus

It all adds up to fun in this activity. Reproduce page 32 for each student. Have her complete each equation on the page by writing the addends in the spaces provided. Then direct her to find the sum and write the numeral in the shaded pancake. If desired, provide each child with a set of brown linking-cube "pancakes" to use as manipulatives for help in solving the problems.

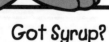

Got Syrup?

Your students will need some after they complete this seriation activity. Give each child a small paper plate and a copy of page 33. Have him color and cut out the pancakes. Then have him stack the pancakes on his plate, from largest to smallest, and glue them down. For added fun, invite the child to drizzle clear-drying glue over the stack of pancakes to resemble syrup.

Butter Buddies

Number-word recognition comes straight off the griddle in this activity. Give each child a copy of page 34. Instruct him to cut out the pats of butter and glue each one onto its corresponding pancake. Finish the page by inviting each child to color his pancakes and illustrate his favorite pancake topping on them. Then wrap up this mini-unit with a pancake party! Make each child a real pancake and invite him to use squeeze butter to label his pancake with his favorite numeral. Now, eat!

Name _____

Pancakes Plus

1.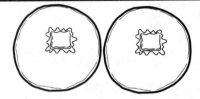

_____ + _____ =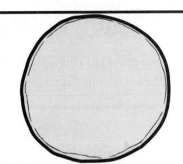

2.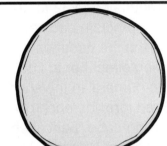

_____ + _____ =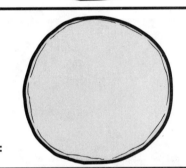

3.

_____ + _____ =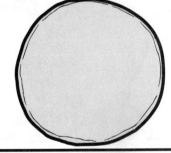

4.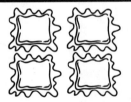

_____ + _____ =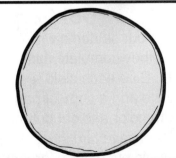

5.

_____ + _____ =

Bonus Box: On the back of your paper, draw the number of pancakes you can eat.

Name ______________________________

Butter Buddies

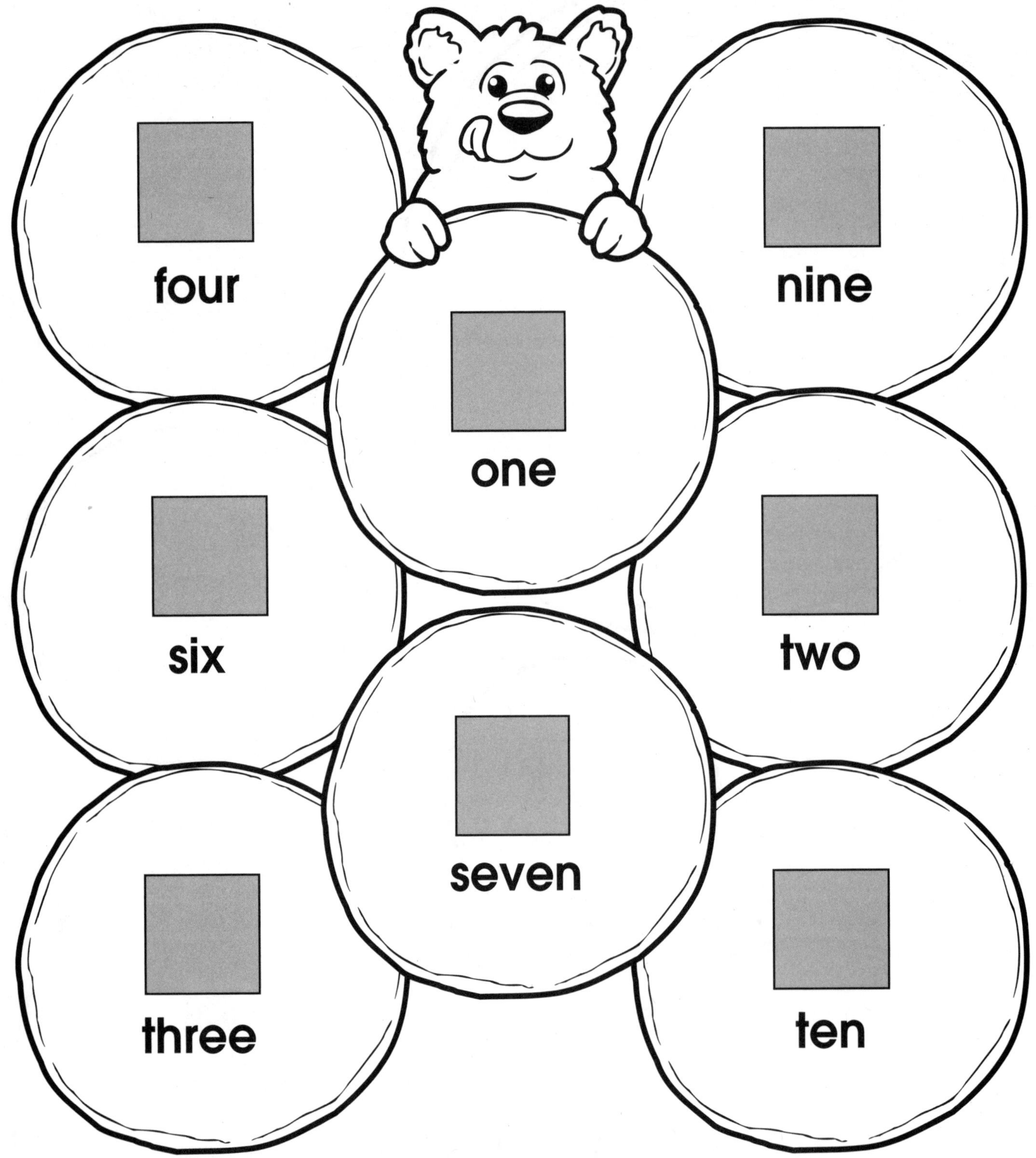
four
nine
one
six
two
seven
three
ten

Bonus Box: Illustrate your favorite topping on these pancakes.

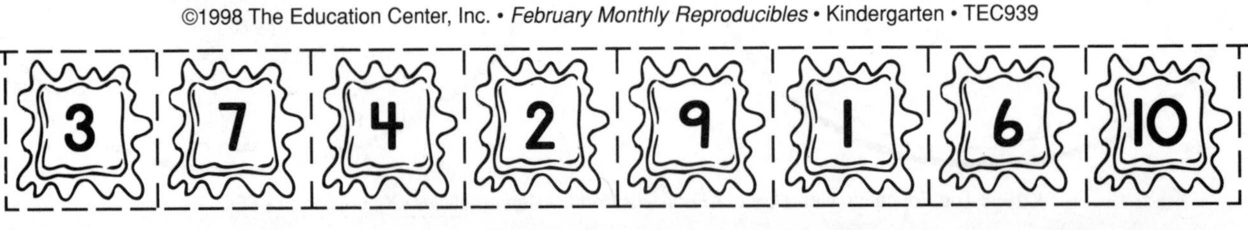
3
7
4
2
9
1
6
10

VALENTINE'S DAY

Enrich your valentine festivities with these lovely activities. Your little Cupids will shoot their arrows right through the hearts of some basic skills in math and language. Happy Valentine's Day!

Love, Love, Love

That's what it's all about in this activity. Duplicate the booklet found on pages 37–39 onto construction paper for each child. Read through the following directions and gather the necessary materials for each child to make the booklet. Have the child cut out his booklet pages and the accompanying pieces. Then assist him in completing the following steps:

Cover: Write your name where indicated. Then decorate the cover with an assortment of heart/valentine stickers and stamps.

Page 1: Glue the lamp piece to the correct space on the page; then color the picture—being careful not to color over the words. Glue one long edge of a 1 1/2" x 4 1/2" piece of fabric to the bed in order to make a flap.

Page 2: Glue the left edge of the paper-bag piece to the page where indicated to make a flap. Color the picture; then fill the shopping cart with food items cut from a discarded magazine.

Page 3: Glue the tree piece to the page as indicated. Make green fingerprinted leaves on the tree; then color the rest of the picture.

Page 4: Color the face and shirt outline to resemble yourself. Glue the heart piece to the page where indicated; then color the rest of the picture.

Once all of the pages are finished, stack the pages in order and staple them together along the left side. Read the booklet aloud; then encourage volunteers to take turns reading the predictable text.

Under the bed?

Next to the cart? 2

Behind the tree? 3

Love is in my heart! 4

Soul Mates

Children's visual-discrimination skills get a real workout here as they try to find and match identical hearts. Cut out several pairs of hearts—each pair from a different sample of wallpaper. Use the hearts in a game of Memory. Then reproduce page 40 as a follow-up activity for independent practice.

A Sweet Treat

It wouldn't be Valentine's Day without something sweet to eat! Gather the ingredients and materials needed for the snack on page 42. To prepare for the activity, slice a piece of pound cake for each child; tint white frosting red or pink; and pour candy toppings (sprinkles, red cinnamon hearts, etc.) into a bowl. Enlarge and reproduce the directions on page 42. Post them at your cooking center and invite each child to visit the center to make a snack. For enrichment, make class copies of page 42 and cut the directions into strips. Give each child a piece of construction paper and instruct him to glue the directions onto the paper in the correct order. Now it's time to nibble!

Let Me Count The Ways!

Count on this activity to entice youngsters to put their hearts into graphing. Give each child a copy of page 41 and ten small counters. Point to the graph at the bottom of the page. Ask a child to name one of the objects represented on the graph. For example, she might say "a heart." Then have each student place a counter on each of the hearts that she finds in the picture. Next have each child count her counters and color the same amount of spaces on the graph. Repeat this procedure for each of the objects on the graph. Wrap up the activity by asking students to compare the groups to see which has the fewest, the most, the same, etc. Count me in!

36

Name _Cindy McDonald_   Valentine's Day
                                                         Graphing
Will You Be Mine?

How many?
Count.
Graph.

	1	2	3	4	5	6	7	8	9	10

Where Is Love?

by _____

Glue fabric here.

Glue lamp here.

Nope!

Under the bed?

1

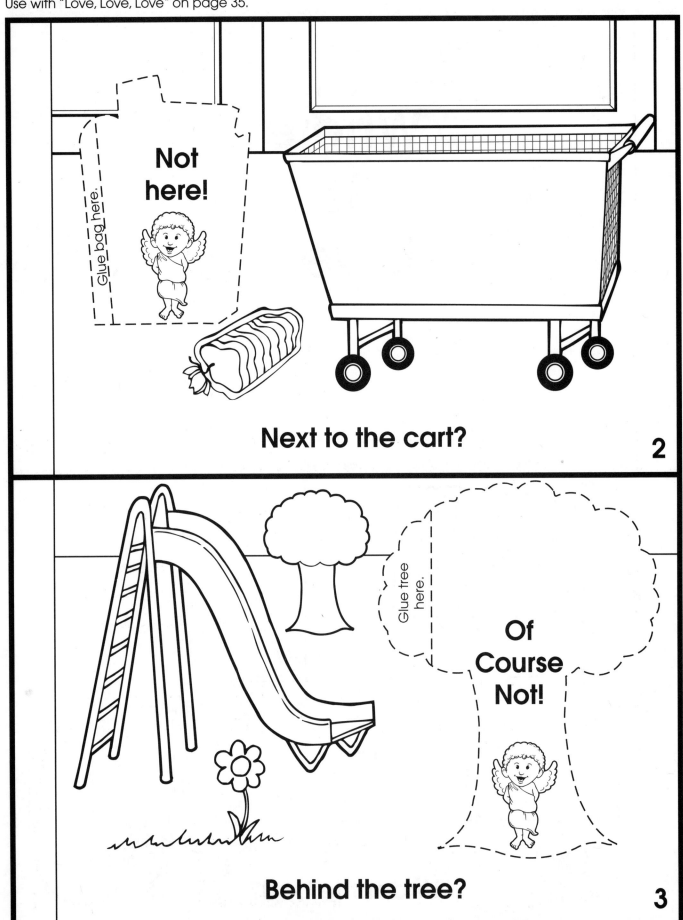

Glue bag here.

Not here!

Next to the cart?

2

Glue tree here.

Of Course Not!

Behind the tree?

3

Glue heart here.

Love is in my heart!

4

Booklet Pattern Pieces
Use with "Love, Love, Love" on page 35.

OATSIES

Soul Mates

Find the two hearts that are alike in each row.
Color them.

©1998 The Education Center, Inc. • *February Monthly Reproducibles* • Kindergarten • TEC939

Name _____

Will You Be Mine?

How many?
Count.
Graph.

	1	2	3	4	5	6	7	8	9	10
(angel)										
(candy)										
(envelope)										
(heart)										

Name _____

You will need:

A Sweet Treat

 heart-shaped
cookie cutter

 plastic knife

 spoon

 paper plate

 slice of pound cake

 tinted frosting

 candy topping

1. Cut a heart shape
from the cake slice.

2. Spread frosting over
the heart.

3. Sprinkle candies
on top.

PRESIDENTS' DAY

Presidents' Day is a day to observe the birthdays of Abraham Lincoln and George Washington as well as to honor all former presidents of the United States. It is celebrated on the third Monday in February. Use the following presidential activities to color your curriculum with a little red, white, and blue!

Flip Your Wig, George!

Change presidents and time periods with just a flip of the wig in this activity. Each child will need two white, construction-paper copies of the pattern on page 44; glue; scissors; crayons or markers; white cotton balls; cotton balls tinted with black powdered tempera paint; yarn; three buttons; and four large wiggle eyes. Direct the child to cut out both patterns, then glue them together back-to-back. On one side have the child depict Abraham Lincoln by coloring the hat black, gluing on two wiggle eyes, gluing on yarn to resemble glasses, drawing a nose and mouth, and gluing on black cotton balls to make his beard. After the glue is dry, flip the paper over and upside down. Instruct the child to portray George Washington on this side by gluing on white cotton to resemble a wig, gluing on two wiggle eyes, drawing a nose and mouth, coloring his shirt blue, and gluing buttons on his shirt. Now there's an outstanding president no matter how you look at it!

Presidential Race

The best part of this race is the learning that takes place along the way! Enlarge, reproduce, and laminate the silhouettes on page 45. Post the silhouettes on an easel where they are accessible to your students. Divide your class into two teams: George's team and Abe's team. Show a child on Abe's team a numeral, shape, letter, sight word, basic addition fact, etc. If the child correctly identifies the symbol (or gives the correct answer), have him use a wipe-off marker to connect the dots between two adjacent stars on Abe's silhouette. If the child doesn't know the answer, the question goes to a member of George's team and vice versa. The first team to trace the entire silhouette of its president is the winner.

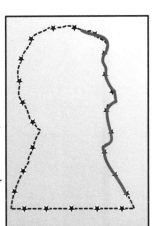
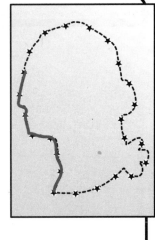

No Cherries, No Pie!

Presidents' Day just wouldn't be complete without sharing the tale of George Washington and the cherry tree. After telling the famous story and discussing *honesty* with your little ones, follow up with this cherry tree project. To prepare, collect a class supply of paper-towel tubes and a supply of red sticky dots. Then duplicate the patterns on page 46 onto white construction paper for each child. To make a cherry tree, fingerpaint the tree pattern green and color the little George pattern. After the paint dries, cut out the tree, little George, and the poem. Glue the poem to the center of the tree; then stick several red-dot cherries to the tree around the poem. Staple the tree to one end of the cardboard-tube trunk. Finish the project by gluing little George behind the tree trunk as indicated.

Pattern
Use with "Flip Your Wig, George!" on page 43.

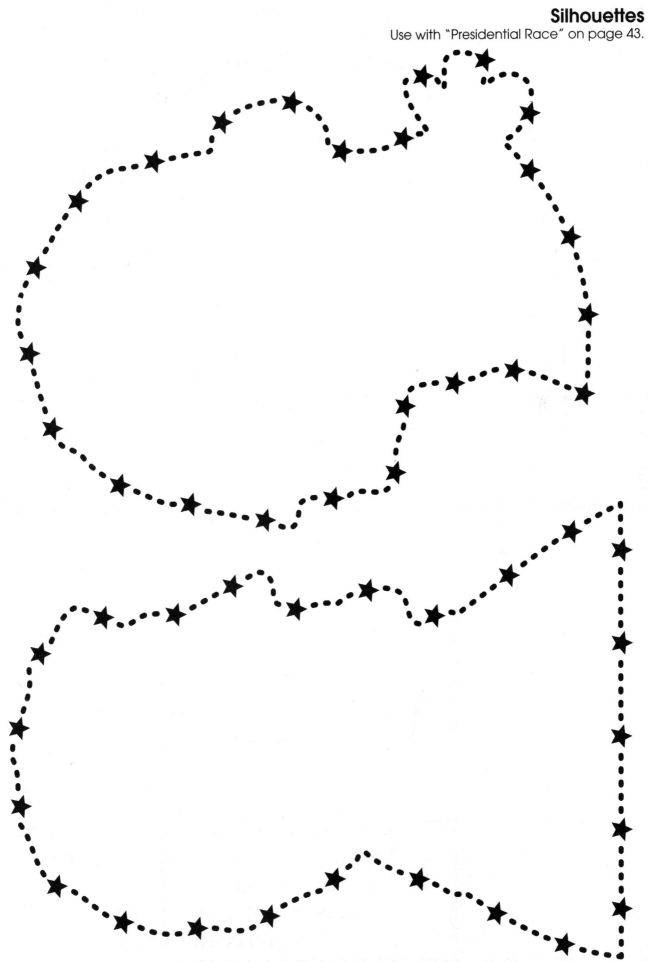

Patterns
Use with "No Cherries,
No Pie!" on page 43.

Glue this tab to back of trunk.

George's father said, "I'm proud of you!
You did not tell a lie.
But now our little tree is gone.
We'll have no cherry pie."

NATIONAL CHERRY MONTH

Three cheers for cherries! They're red, they're juicy, they're tart, and they're oh, so tasty! Use cherries to add flavor to your curriculum with these fun ideas.

Just "Ripe"!

Beginning sounds by the bushel—that's what students will get with this reproducible. Give each child a copy of page 48. Go over the names of the objects pictured on the cherries. Then instruct each child to look at each cherry and color it red if the pictured object starts with *ch* or color it green if the pictured object doesn't start with *ch*. Encourage the child to color the rest of the reproducible. Then give her a small handful of cinnamon red hots and have her glue them onto the paper to trace the **ch** label on the basket. When the activity is complete, invite the child to "ch-ch-chew" on the leftover candies!

What A Good Pick!

Enlist cherries to help with classroom management. Mount a large tree-shaped cutout on a wall within students' reach. Cut out a class supply of red, construction-paper cherries. Then label each cherry with a different child's name. Attach the cherries facedown on the tree. Whenever you need a student helper, simply pick a cherry from the tree!

Which Cherry Next?

What can you do with a bagful of cherry-flavored jelly beans and an overhead projector? Teach ordinal numbers, of course! Arrange five of the jelly beans in a row on your overhead projector. Use the following rhyme to encourage student participation. Continue repeating the rhyme until each child has had a turn to munch on a jelly bean. For more advanced students, use ten jelly beans instead of five.

[Five] juicy cherries looking so fine.
[Child's name] ate the [fourth] one in the line!

Last verse:
One juicy cherry looking so fine.
This one looks best because it's mine, mine, mine! *(Teacher eats the last one.)*

Just "Ripe"!

Color the cherries with the *ch* sound **red.**

Color the other cherries **green.**

©1998 The Education Center, Inc. • *February Monthly Reproducibles* • Kindergarten • TEC939

Post Office · Adventures ·

With all of the valentine exchanges taking place, February is a great time of year for talking about the post office. The mail carrier can deliver lots of opportunities for first-class learning. So use these postal activities that carry our special stamp of approval!

Neither Rain Nor Snow…

Weather may not be a factor in mail delivery but directions are! Give each child a copy of page 51 and a crayon. Challenge youngsters to help the mail carrier find his way to the mailbox by following these directions.

Directions:
1. Go left to the C.
2. Go up to the G.
3. Go left to the K.
4. Go up to the B.
5. Go right to the X.
6. Go down to the P.
7. Go right to the I.
8. Go up to the V.
9. Go left to the F.
10. Go up to the Q.
11. Go left to the L.
12. Go up to the T.
13. Go right to the D.
14. Go up to the O.
15. Go left to the mailbox!

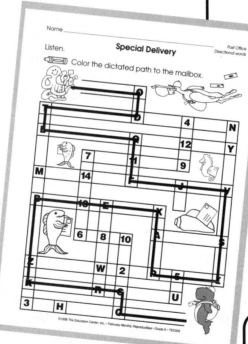

Name _____

Listen.   **Special Delivery**   Post Office Directional words

Color the dictated path to the mailbox.

©1998 The Education Center, Inc. • February Monthly Reproducibles • Grade K • TEC939

If time allows, have each child use another color of crayon to follow a different set of directions from student volunteers.

Pen Pals

Invite students to discuss how they communicate with friends far away. Do any of them write letters? Discuss the process that a letter goes through to reach its destination. If possible, show pictures from a reference book. Then make a copy of page 52 for each child. Have her color, cut out, and sequence this simplified version of the mail process.

Rabbit starts with *R.*

A Letter For Me!

Getting a letter in the mail is always fun. Collect a class supply of envelopes. Into each envelope, insert a picture of a different (familiar) object. Designate one student as the Mail Carrier. Have her deliver a piece of mail to each child. On the child's turn, have him open his letter, show the picture to the rest of the group, and name the beginning sound of the object. After everyone has had a turn, collect the envelopes and invite another Mail Carrier to deliver the mail. This time have students practice another skill, such as naming the ending sound, naming a rhyming word, or naming another object that begins like the pictured object. To follow up this activity, give each child a copy of page 53. Instruct the child to look at each picture, then color the stamp that belongs on its envelope. A stamp for the beginning sound and a stamp for the ending sound are included with each envelope so that you can choose the skill for each child, depending on his abilities.

Service With A Smile!

Send this activity to your students C.O.D.—that's "Comprehend On Delivery"—to practice listening comprehension. Make a copy of page 54 for each child. Have him listen to and complete these oral directions:

1. Draw a blue hat on the mail carrier's head.
2. Color his pants red.
3. Draw red and blue stripes on his shirt.
4. Give the mail carrier a mustache.
5. Draw a mailbag over the mail carrier's shoulder.
6. Draw two letters in one of his hands and three letters in the other.
7. Color half of his mail truck blue.
8. Write your name on the mailbox on the left.
9. Color the mailboxes the same.
10. Finish the picture by drawing your favorite kind of weather.

Name _____

Special Delivery

Listen.

Color the dictated path to the mailbox.

		O			
T		D		4	N
L		Q		12	Y
	7		11	9	
M	14		F	J	V
B	13	E		X	
				A	S
	6	8	10		
Z		W	2	P	5	I
K		R	G		U	
3	H		C		

Pen Pals

🖍 Color.   ✂ Cut.   Sequence.   🧴 Glue.

1	2	3	4	5	6

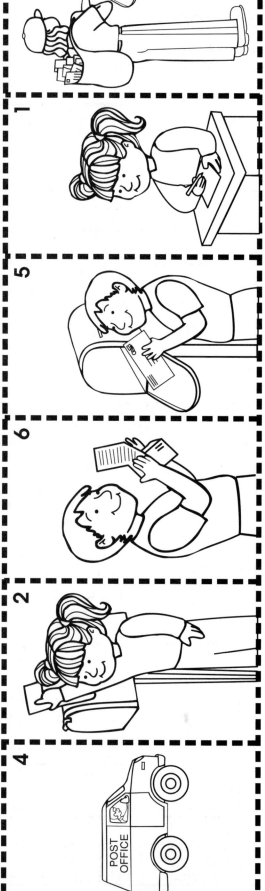

Name _____

Stamp It!

Say the word.

 Color the correct stamp.

Name

Service With A Smile!

Listen and do.

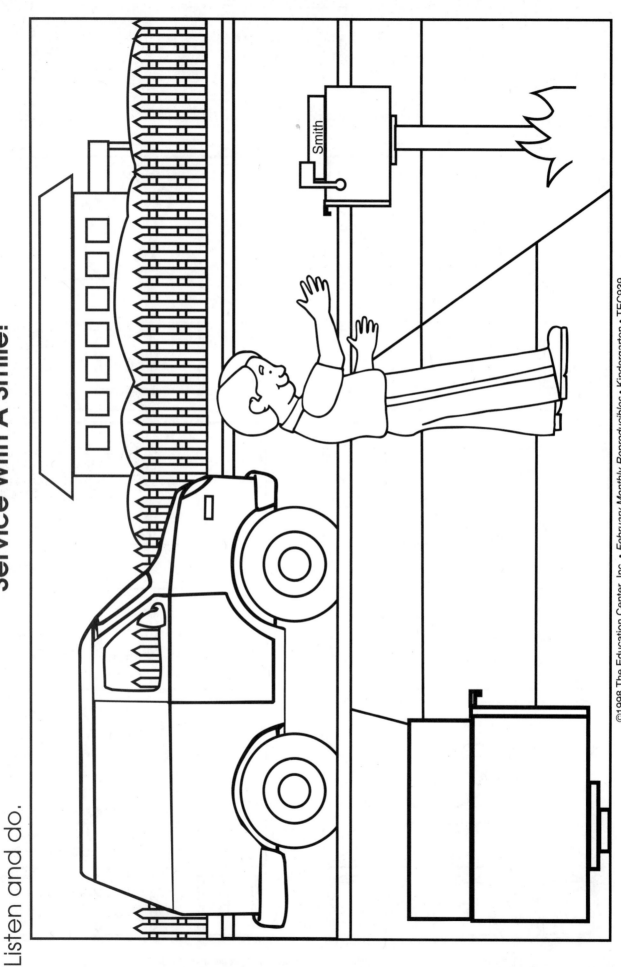

Smith

AMERICAN HEART MONTH

Your youngsters will be pumped after completing these "heart-y" activities on one of the most important muscles in our bodies.

Good For Your Heart

Lowering the risk of heart disease is in the bag—the grocery bag, that is. Bring in a bagful of heart-healthful and not-so-healthful foods, such as fresh vegetables and fruits, salty chips, skim milk, cookies, candy, eggs, and butter. Take one item out of the bag at a time. Discuss whether or not the food is good for your heart. Does it contain a lot of fat? Does it have a lot of salt? Then sort the items into two respective groups. After the discussion give volunteers a chance to name other good and bad foods for the heart. Then use copies of page 57 as an activity to extend this idea. Here's to your hearts!

Have A Healthy Heart

Keeping your heart in good shape is as easy as 1, 2, 3 with this craft project. Give each child a construction-paper copy of the patterns on page 58 and four 7-inch lengths of yarn. After discussing ways to keep your heart in tip-top shape, have each child color and cut out the patterns. To construct the healthy-heart mobile, use a hole puncher to make seven holes where indicated. Tie each healthy-heart tip to one of the bottom holes with a different piece of yarn. Then tie one end of the last piece of yarn to the top of the heart for hanging. Encourage youngsters to hang their mobiles at home to serve as reminders to be heart smart!

How's Your Heart Rate?

Show youngsters that they can measure how fast their hearts are pumping by feeling their pulses on their necks or wrists. Explain that the more physically or emotionally active a person is, the faster his heart rate will be. Demonstrate this by having each child feel his pulse for ten seconds while sitting still. Then have him feel it again after two or three minutes of jogging in place. After discussing actions that could cause fast and slow heart rates, have each child complete the reproducible activity on page 56.

How's Your Heart Rate?

Color.

Cut.

Glue.

Fast	**Slow**

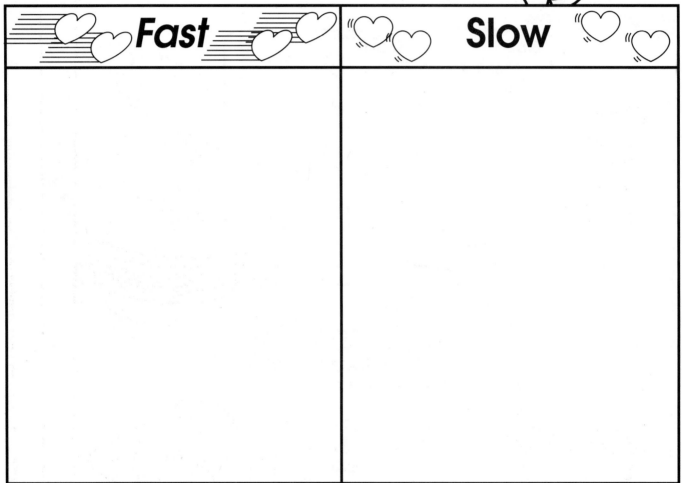

Good For Your Heart!

Color only the foods that are good for your heart.

Patterns

Use with "Have A Healthy
Heart" on page 55.

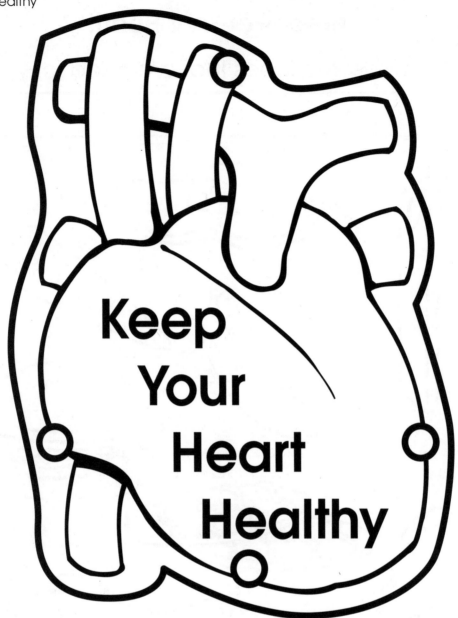

Keep
Your
Heart
Healthy

Eat right. | Don't smoke. | Exercise.

A WHALE OF A TIME!

Look! Out in the ocean! It's a whale—whoopee! Have a whale of a good time using these activities to complement your cetacean studies.

Spout It Out!

Here's a great craft project to follow up a singing of "Baby Beluga" from Raffi's album *Baby Beluga* (Troubadour Records). Duplicate the patterns on page 61 onto white construction paper for each child. Have each child paint or fingerpaint two-thirds of a piece of 9" x 12" construction paper blue to represent the ocean. Then have him cut out the two beluga whales and the strip from page 61. After the paint is dry, instruct the child to glue the bigger beluga on the paper so that her blowhole is at the water's surface and then glue the baby beluga anywhere he chooses. Give the child two small wiggle eyes to glue onto the whales. Cut two 3-inch vertical slits above the bigger beluga's blowhole as shown. Help the child thread the strip of paper through these slits. Encourage him to gently pull the strip through the slits to make the beluga spout. Whoosh!

Big And Little

Whales come in different sizes, just like our alphabet. Put a "whale-acious" twist on letter discrimination with this puzzle. Give each child a copy of page 60, and have her *lightly* color the spaces with lowercase letters black and the spaces with uppercase letters blue. If she completes the activity correctly, an orca whale will appear. But don't tell; it's a secret!

Cetacean Classification

Your little marine biologists will be determining which whale is which in this classification activity. Duplicate page 62 for each child. Read aloud the directions so that each child understands what to do. (You may even want to guide children through one direction at a time.) For added fun, play a recording of actual whale songs (found at most nature stores) while children are working.

Name

Where's The Whale?

Color the spaces with **lowercase** letters **black.**

Color the spaces with **uppercase** letters **blue.**

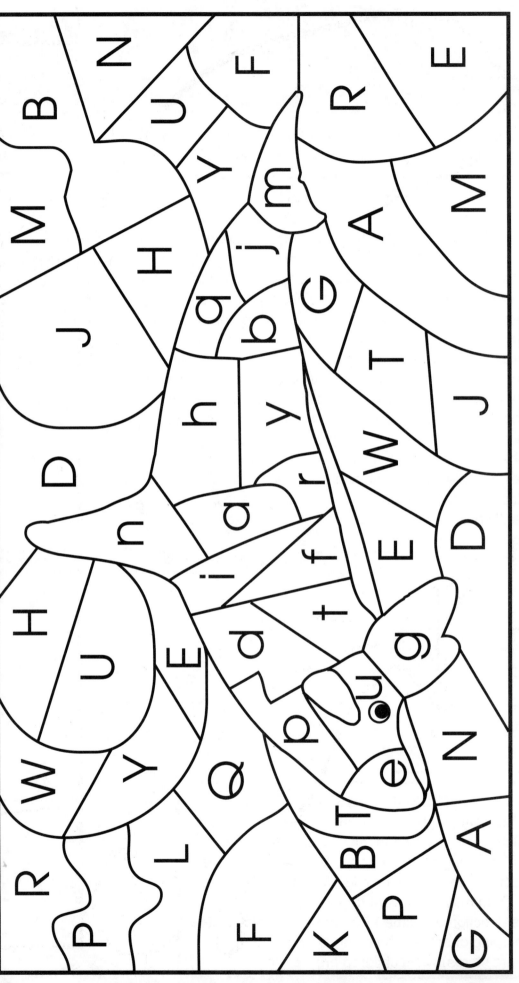

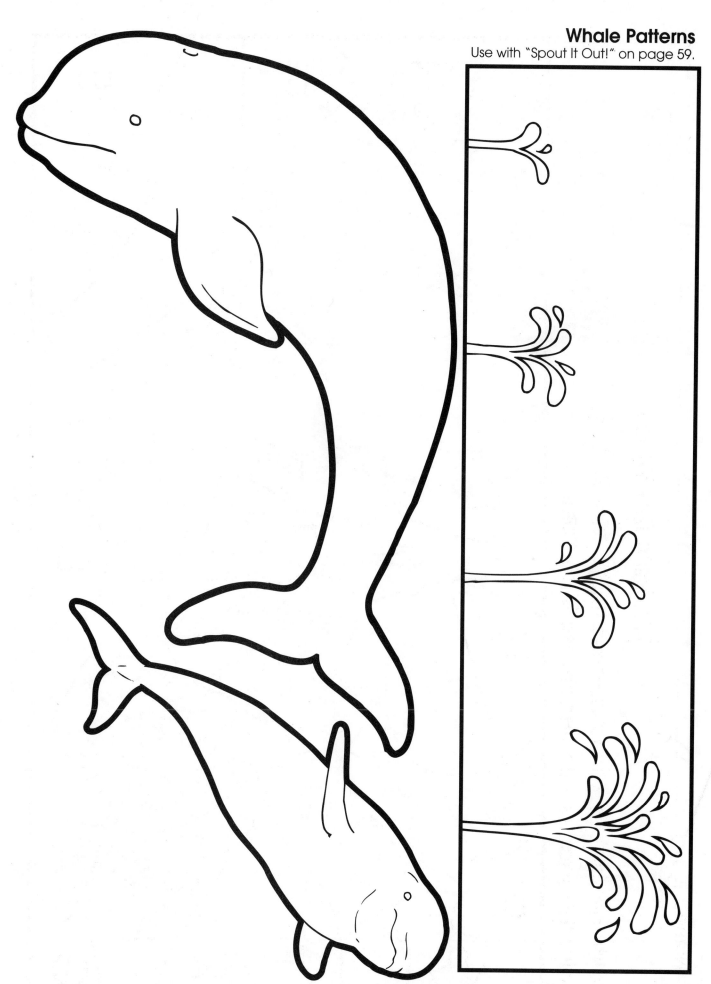

Whale Patterns
Use with "Spout It Out!" on page 59.

Name _____

Whales
Classification

A Sea Of Whales

Draw a red ⬭ around each 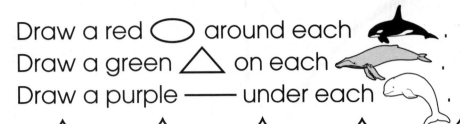 .
Draw a green △ on each .
Draw a purple —— under each .

Bonus Box: Draw your favorite type of whale on the back of this paper.

READ TO YOUR CHILD DAY

"Show your kids you love them: read to them." That's the motto of this special day, held annually on February 14. Take this opportunity to promote reading to children with the following ideas.

It Takes The Whole Village

Encourage parents, grandparents, older siblings, and other caregivers to share the joy of reading with little ones. Collect a class supply of inexpensive trade books to use as rewards for completing this activity. Then reproduce the reading chart on page 64 for each child. Have each child take her chart home and color a box for each book that a grown-up reads to her. Invite the child to return her filled chart and exchange it for a new book.

Literacy Letter

Send copies of the following note home to inform parents and caregivers of the benefits of reading with their children. For a special touch, attach a small plastic bag of Hershey's® Hugs® and Kisses® to each note as a reminder to make the most of these few minutes of quality time every day!

Read To Your Child Day– February 14

Show your kids you love them: read to them.

(Then share some hugs and kisses!)

©1998 The Education Center, Inc.
February Monthly Reproducibles • Kindergarten • TEC939

Reading to your child
- develops phonemic awareness
- teaches the sequence of events
- promotes growth in vocabulary
- builds memory skills
- gives new experiences
- reinforces basic concepts such as time, place, and size
- stimulates the imagination
- provides a reading role model
- nurtures your relationship

Please

Color a box for each book read.

Name

Read To Me